This book is dedicated to my Radha Krishan, whom I see in every individual living on this planet, as all this knowledge & information has been gathered from them and has been offered for healing of his disciples.

My father was alive when I started writing this book, and today I can complete this book with his blessings only.

Index

ONE LIFE, ONE THOUGHT

OMSHREE AKARSHANA

not make any representations or warranties of any kind, express or implied, including but not limited to the implied warranties of merchantability, fitness for a particular purpose. The Publisher and Editor shall not be liable whatsoever for any errors, omissions, whether such errors or omissions result from negligence, accident, or any other cause or claims for loss or damages of any kind, including without limitation, indirect or consequential loss or damage arising out of use, inability to use, or about the reliability, accuracy or sufficiency of the information contained in this book.

Preface

Today, the people of this World are running in a rat race.

Some people are running to gather those possessions which they feel will turn around their life.

Some people possess everything, but certainly they do not have time to enjoy their possession. They are also running for something else, which they do not have.

People are set on a journey which they don't know, where to end and when to end.

They put hardest efforts to get something in life and most of their actions end up in vain.

People are suffering in relationships, scarcities, deficiencies, negativities and limiting beliefs.

This book is, therefore, conceptualize to help them with what they want.

This book contains suggestive dialogue to tell the concept of thoughts.

One can expect anything good in one's life if he follows the suggestive practices in this book.

You can rely on my words, that I have personally felt outcomes of these practices, which brought quality in my life.

This book contains stories and instances to give you a clear perspective of what life can bring for them.

I would request you to go through the suggestions made in the book and to create a belief in the natural system, so that they can let their dreams come true.

I am looking forward to seeing if this book can make a small positive change in somebody' life.

I would be keen to know and be available to listen to the contact details mentioned somewhere in the book.

Happy reading

Yours
Omshree Akarshana

alias
Omm Agrawal

Prologue

One Life, One Thought
Our life is an outcome of our thoughts.

This is one Life by virtue of something good, we have been brought here.

It is said that a soul gets the life of a human being after passing many lives of various creatures, I don't know what the truth is.

After thousands of stages, one gets a Life of a human being.

Don't you think?

Being a human is being the most sophisticated creature on earth.

Does any other being have a brain like us?

Does any other being can talk, walk and act so easily like us?

With so much diversity, Human being is an ultimate machinery, much complex, much advanced.

This advancement came out of evolution over a period.

This human machine has every feature.

This can listen, see, speak, think, understand, communicate unlike many other creatures.

Most important organ of it is BRAIN which can create wonders of the World.

All inventions and discoveries are brought to you by this human brain.

It has immense power and capabilities.

We can easily compare human beings with mobiles and computers.

Yes, there is a variety in quality of human beings as well,
Some human beings can do one task while others cannot do it. This could be a similarity with mobile phones and computers. Wherein, high end mobile phones and computers have more features, whereas low end ones are cheaper with limited features.

Now coming to the point.

The ultimate thing with the human brain is its *thoughts* which make it a version.
A higher version has higher quality of thoughts, accounted thoughts, clear and focused thoughts.
This version of the human being has full control over his life and destiny.
He can seek anything whatever he wants and well within desired time.
The lower version has a variation based on quality of thought.
A criminal's mind is always a clutter of disastrous thoughts.

Like computers, a human version can be upgraded by changing the way of his thinking.

This book therefore tells us how these thoughts can change our life for a better one.

How we can identify wrong thoughts and let the odd man out.

How we can include better thoughts in our life.

This book also contains practice sessions to let everybody understand the form and the ways of how to do it.

I
An Idea Can Change Your Life

****

100 years of life is not enough for one to change & it took a nick of a second for others to decide their fate.

Mohandas would not have become Mahatma, if he was not thrown at Pietermaritzburg Railway Platform of South Africa addressing him as a "Black" and a "slave".

On the night of June 7'1893, a British trained young lawyer Mohandas was traveling through a train in South Africa.

He took a first-class compartment ticket for his journey from the station.

The compartment was a "White Only" compartment wherein only English man could travel which Mohandas missed to see.

Later, an Englishman saw a black sitting in the compartment.

Mohandas was forced to leave the seat and instructed to move to the general compartment.

He refused to leave the seat and was thrown out of the train along with his luggage despite his resistance.

That time, he was in South Africa,

In a nick of a second, he understood that he is a slave and is living in a slave country, he acted upon the thought and spared around 20 years of his life for betterment of Africans,

He then came to India, to let Indians lead Independence.

He developed his principals of peaceful resistance "Satyagraha" and led India people to mobilize them against discriminatory rule of British.

The basic crux behind telling this story is to raise the question that -

Is that Mohan das did not knew that he is a slave, and living in a slave country, before happening of train incidence in South Africa?

Mohandas was born in 1869, in a rich family, his father was Diwan (Chief Minister) of Por bander near Rajkot, Gujarat.

His mother was a religious lady. He left India at the age of 19, to study Barrister at law in London.

He came back after successfully completing his studies.

The incident took place in 1893 when he was 24 years old.

He already knew that India is under British rule, he went to England for studies and became Barrister.

He didn't practiced law in India and went to South Africa.

Certainly, he was brought up in a rich family and wanted to improve the status of his family and earn a name & fame.

Probably, slavery of Englishman never bothered him.

Instead, Many of Englishman were his friends. But this train incidence changed his thought process and a common man Mohandas turned "Mahatma"

This is the power of thought.

An idea can change your life,
it is important, how you take it.

Issac Newton

In June'1661, Issac Newton was sitting and reading a book under an apple tree when an apple from the tree fell next to him, and the idea of earth's gravitational force came into being.

Before this, it was understood that objects fall because of their specific gravity and earth's gravitation pull was never thought of.

GautamBuddha

Siddhartha took birth in a Kings' family, his mother died after giving him birth.

He was brought up in extreme luxuries.

He had a beautiful wife Yasodhara and a son Rahul.

His realization that he, like anybody else, will be subject to all forms of human sufferings viz, diseases, ageing and ultimately death.

This thought took him into crisis. He left home at the age of 29, in search of the truth.

There are lots of examples of one thought changing the mind and ultimately destiny.

People say, "They are unhappy with their life". "They are unhappy with what is going on". etcetera

I want to take you through a thought.

Let you find yourself amid a river. The river has ample water and is flowing at its full speed.

What can you do?

Option 1-
Let's you drive against the flow of the river to save yourself from drowning.

This is an act which requires maximum push against water,

and the more resistance you give to the power, the more energy you will require to through away the water,

The more you put the energy into this task, the more you will feel pain.

You will win if you can bear the resistance to getting out of the water.

For that, you should have sufficient power which shall not be less than the push given by river water,

and you are expected to bear this pain.
In case you broke, you will be drowned.

Option 2-
Another option is to let yourself flow freely in the direction of the river water. This is the stage of least resistance, minimum energy is required in this act and therefore, there is no pain.

So, Option 2 is comfortable once you know that the river water will not drown you.

This is the story of life.

We are all flowing in a river, a river of time. We always try to change the system, change things, change people resulting in resistance and pain.
We try to make things as per our choice and since we do not have capacity and power to change, we fail.
Instead of changing the system, things, or people, can we change ourselves?

Because

It is only I who has the right to myself. It is the "I" who can change myself.

And believe it or not, try it.

Changing Me will instantly change the way you
see the WORLD.
Because

**The world is what I see, it is
just a mirror of my thoughts.**

***

II
Power Of Your Thoughts

Let's have a story.

"A Saint was walking on a roadside towards its destination, evening time and the night was about to happen.

No streetlights, no houses nearby, jungle all around, road cannot be seen from far. He was walking, and walking, and walking.

Suddenly, he saw a tree by the roadside, and it was approximately dinner time, he was also feeling some hunger, he was tired too, so he stayed there, for the night.

By the time he was settling himself at the place, cleaning it, placing a mat for resting and checking his bag for any food item lying in it, he drank some water available in the pot.

A thought arrived in his mind giving him a good feel of an awesome meal,

He uttered, O God, if I get an awesome meal here at this moment of time, would be quite enjoyable, the meal should have sweets, various dishes, various types of breads etc.

By God's grace, instantly, a food platter arrived in actual, somebody brought this, we will not go into who brought this, he was astonished and felt happy.

Without applying mind, he started eating the plate and completed the meal in very little time.

As soon as the meal was completed, he thought of having a good liquor, if it happens, would be better, he murmured.

Again, a pot filled with liquor of his choice arrived, which he drank and planned for sleep.

He was very happy as he got what he wanted and very instantly. He was amazed at his good luck.

While thinking this, he was trying to sleep, suddenly, he saw an image formed in darkness which was a scary one, it was an image of a Devil, the devil was a big shaped, about 10 times of the size of the saint, dark in color, he was slowly coming towards the saint trying to terrorize him.

The saint got sweat out of fear and terror. He was palpitating and threatened.

He thought that the scary devil wants to kill him, and over a period, this thought became so strong to believe that the devil will certainly kill him.

Out of anguish, threat and fear, the saint died.

Moral of the story is -

Positive thoughts brought good things for the saint to enjoy, but a single negative thought sacrificed his life.

> ***Thoughts have the power to take you anywhere, just focus on positive ones.***

Thinking Process - How it happens?

From the point of time of entering a thought in your mind for doing an action, till the time of start of that action.

Do you think, what happens?

During this small period, your mind processes the action, visualize it, repeat it. It does this process so many times and concludes with the result.

So, the mind mentally does the very same task, many times, which he is about to do.

So, before the start of action, the mind knows the complete process and even the result of the action.

Therefore, without doing anything physically, your mind knows the result of the action & to your surprise, the physical result is always same as the result predicted by mind before doing that action.

__The actual result of a physical action is same as that of result obtained during thinking process.__

For example, for those having a spouse, let's suppose, your spouse requested you to make a coffee for her. Before physically going in the kitchen and starting to make the coffee. Observe what happens in your mind.

Your mind takes you to walk through the whole process, like you are going to the kitchen, lighting the gas stove, putting a pan on the stove, pouring water in the bowl, water is boiling, putting ingredients and milk etc. and now the coffee is ready.

So, before reaching the kitchen, your mind takes you for a walkthrough of the whole process of making a coffee and to your surprise the physical coffee is prepared in the same way.

***

III

You Wish, You Get

***

You wish, you get.

Experienced people say, whatever you will wish, you will get from the Universe.

I am saying they are wrong.

It is in built in the system.

It is mandatory that "Whatever you wish, you certainly get", no matter any circumstance.

Since the time of our birth, nature has provided us the feature to get what we wish, and this happens till the last moment, we live and it continues even after death, when we are simply a soul and waiting to take new birth.

We are created by nature, and we are in sync with it.

We are a composite of mind, body, and soul, where soul is an energy source which is in sync with nature and never dies, it only changes body.

Right from the beginning, it's the soul who decides whether to take birth, even the womb of the mother is decided by it.

During our whole life, we get what we had thought in the past, on any day before the happening of the instance, good or bad.

Remember, anything that happened to you, had been in your thoughts before- Yes, it was.

Same way, every good thing happened to you, had been in your thoughts before- Of course, yes.

What we generally think,

Something has happened to me, was a matter of chance and there is no connection between my thoughts and happening of the event.

I am saying just reverse of that,

My dear friend, the event happened because of your thought. If you would not have thought, the incidence would not have occurred.

You can review your past and identify at least 10 instances which you thought in the past and have happened...you can put on a paper.

Sample instances

1. You might have got ill some day because it was in your thought to get ill to take off from the work.
2. Your friend ditched because you thought once that he/she might give you a ditch.
3. Some of your close relative got ill or died because it was in your thought in the past.
4. You got a beautiful house or a vehicle of your choice or any of your choice fulfilled because you ever had a thought to have it.
5. You got new clothes because you thought that you should.

6. You were not good at studies, because you thought you could not.
7. You were very good at your studies because you always thought you could do it.
8. You are earning good money in your job or profession, because you once thought you would get it.
9. You are living a life of scarcity because you thought you must live a life like that.
10. Lastly, you are dead because you thought you could not survive.

So, shall we conclude with the connotation, whatever we are thinking today, good, or bad, whether it will be our future.

The answer is-

Of course, yes
What to do?

Start thinking good, to create a better future.

At least stop thinking badly, so to avoid a bad one.

Let's work on our thinking process,
Let's sit in silence for at least 15 minutes, you can sit for more time if you can.
Let's breathe slowly but deeply.

Let's focus on our thoughts, may be good, may be weird,

Let them come and let them go,

Smile on every thought,

Make it a practice,

Slowly you would be conscious of the quality of thoughts coming and going.

After doing around 10-15 sittings, you would be conscious of the quality of your thoughts and a good one starts keeping with you and bad ones automatically starts eliminating by nature.

This practice will improve the quality of our thoughts and certainly our life will change for the better.

***

IV
Your Body, Your Vehicle

***

Do you have a car or a bike.

Do you know, how to ride it…Great, you know how to ride a bike.

So, you ride it very often. Probably, yes.

What happens when your vehicle's tire gets flat.

What happens when the vehicle does not start.

What happens when it is sounding more than normal, and the average km run per liter is less than normal.

Fuss, all these are problems which we do not want to face, and we do not allow any vehicle in our life which creates a trouble like this.

Probably, your vehicle troubles you once in a year and still it is a problem, even if it troubles you once in five years, still you will not accept it.

Remember, you regularly send your vehicle for oiling, servicing, cleaning to the service station and spend money to care for this.

Now, Let's think about another vehicle which you got by nature.

YOUR BODY.

What do you do with it?

Every day, in the evening, when you reach home, your body becomes so tired that you can't afford to bear a small spoon. In the morning, the body does not allow you to leave the bed and it look like that the whole night, you did not sleep, or you slept but your body did not take rest.

After every few days, you get a fever or so, sometimes, stomachache or sometimes backache troubles you.

If you do not walk for some days, your legs create numbness or pain.

If nothing creates pain, your mind starts chattering,

Multiple thoughts come to your mind connecting your past and future.

If sitting idle for the whole day, your mind takes you to the events of the past or future, you have planned for taking rest and the whole lot day goes resting, and still at the end of the day, you feel tired.

What was the problem?

Why there was no rest, even when you are resting throughout the day, without leaving the bed except for going to washrooms?

What happened is that,

Your physical body was resting, but your mind was not at rest.

Do you want this type of vehicle which every now and then gets you in trouble,

or

Are you ok to continue with this vehicle?

Oh no, I am NOT telling you to leave it, certainly not.

I just want to take you to the thought that because of our daily stressful life, we have made this vehicle troublesome.

Our spiritual body is built of our mind, our body and our soul and these three unite to form a spiritual body.

Beautiful mind, beautiful body, and a beautiful soul, all together, create beautiful thoughts and thus a beautiful future is made.

***

V
Mind, Body, and Soul

Physically we are one entity i.e., one body.
Spiritually, we are three entities tied together.
Body is physical, mind resides in the physical brain and soul resides near the physical Heart.
All the three united, we become one.

We are built by nature in a way that if we do any task by synchronizing all the three entities together, viz, mind, body and soul, task will be successfully completed,

But, if the task is executed leaving any one entity out of three, certainly we would fail.

THINK

Now, see what happens in actual.

Situation No. 1

Let's take an instance, where you have forgotten your mobile, you kept it at some place and now you cannot memorize where it was kept.

What do you do?

You will call on your mobile from some other's phone. Now, you have come to know that the phone was left one hour before, and you do not even remember where and how it was left?

What is this?
This is a simple example of multitasking.

Your mind was not in sync with your body when the body left the mobile. So, your mind did not recall it as it was busy doing some other tasks.
Your mind was doing some other tasks when the body was leaving the mobile to the forgotten place. This is an act of no sync between your mind and your body.

Situation No. 2

Whenever we like to sleep at night, we go to bed to sleep.

Many times, it happens that we are tired, but we do not get sleep as something, or the other is running in our mind.

Many a time, we wake up in the morning but our body or the mind do not let us awake, and we feel a greater need for extra sleep.

What happened?

When the body was going to sleep, the mind was not ready for it. This is the reason we slept physically but not mentally. This generally happens with people who spend a lot of time on social media, mobile, internet, watching movies and television etc., or the people who are worried about some recent act happened with them.

What is the problem?

Simple, all these examples showing your mind and your body are not in synchronization. Whatever your body is doing, mind is not cooperating and vice versa.

This problem of absence of sync between your mind, body and soul is not a recent one, nor it is happening in a one-off instance,

This problem is recurring in nature and has been happening for many years.

Therefore, this absence of sync has now become a problem.

Problem of a BAD HABIT.

Many of our psychological, mental, and physical diseases are because of this wrong habit.

HABIT, Is this HABIT?

Yes, this is Habit and certainly a bad habit and nothing else.

How are Habits formed?

Habits are formed after doing repeated thoughts / action over a period, Habits can be good or bad. Bad Habits needs to be corrected.

> *For my thoughts to work, My Mind, Body and Soul shall be in sync.*

What to do?

Today onwards, let's practice to-do, one task at one point of time.

Complete the first task then take another one.

Do not become multitasking.

Being multitasking is not an appreciation which generally is misunderstood,

It is a mere bad habit. Let's leave it.

While starting one task, tell yourself like this-

O' my mind, O' my body and O' my soul, I am starting this task, please be in sync.

Always keep your hands and your eyes in contact as much as possible.

Like in situation no. 1.

When the mobile was being kept at one place by the body, we had to tell ourselves that-- *my mind, my body, and my soul, I am putting this mobile at this desk.*

In the same way in situation no.2

While going to bed, we must reach there some 15-20 minutes before sleep leaving all distraction material like social media etc. and saying to ourselves-
my mind, my body, and my soul, I am going to sleep.

What will be the effect?

This will have positive effect on our personality. We will start living in the present and in a conscious state of action. We will get deep sleep in the night and wake up in the morning leaving the bed easily.

We know, there are serious repercussions of not having good sleep over a period. Short term effects could be drowsiness, physical inactivity in day-to-day life which later turns to become stress, anxiety, depression and converts to diabetes, cholesterol, heart failure, high blood pressure etc.

So, let's start living a life with our mind, body and soul in sync, A conscious life and A happy life.

***

VI
Behavior & Habits- 21 days Challenge

***

Our mind consists of 100 billion neurons which are tied together to form a bond. These neurons are hard wired by our thoughts over a period, and therefore, we think in a particular fashion.

This is the reason why different people perceive the same situation differently.

Take an example-

"Two friends were walking on the way, a car rushed from near and hit the dirt which suddenly fell on their clothes. The two friends reacted differently. First one, abused the driver and tried to stop the car to hit him, the other friend was cool enough convincing the first that this is unintentional on the part of car driver, and they can leave the matter now."

"People are hard wired by brain neurons to understand that Hard Work pays and to earn money, name, fame, position, we have to Hard work patiently."

"A labor is hard wired by his brain neurons that he will get Rs 300 after full day hard work in scorching summer days."

"A medical practitioner is hard wired by his brain neurons that he will get Rs 500 after seeing a patient."

"An employee is hard wired by his brain neurons to get fixed sum of money at the end of the month, whatever work he does."

Repeated thoughts build hard wired neurons over a period, thus building our behavior to react in a particular situation.

Behaviors and Habits are different to each other in the way that Habits are repetitive actions and behaviors are reaction on the impulse of the situation. But from the perspective of thoughts, both are outcome of repeated thoughts of similar nature over a period.

Great behaviors and good habits can be cultivated by rewiring the neurons.

A thought can become behavior if it is repeated regularly for at least 21 days.

By repeating selected acts daily for 21 days, one can change his behavior and habits and thus can change his future.

***

VII
Theory of Spiral

***

Let's observe our daily life.

Day starts in the morning.

Observe when you wake up in the morning, what do you do?

Observe the first thought coming to your mind.

Surely, that will be connected in any way with any of the events that happened in the past.

All day thoughts will be connected in the same way and life goes on thinking about the past or dreaming about the future. These are "circular" thoughts.

These thoughts could be negative, leading us to anguish and depression.

Our life is caught up in circular thoughts like this.

A tire moves around the center and if a force is put on the circle in horizontal direction, it moves forward.

If you trace the path of the tire after putting pressure over it would be a Spiral and not circular.

Circular thought process leads us nowhere.

.

From the understanding point of view,

Bringing Spiral Thought process will take you forward in the direction of the thought.

Having positive and growth-oriented thoughts daily, especially in the morning, will turn our thought process from Circular to Spiral.

If we cannot do much, at least do the following-

- When you wake up in the morning, observe your first thought.
- It should not be negative.
- If it is, please eliminate it.
- Shift your focus to a positive and a happy one.
- Feel good and pay gratitude.

Activity

Let's select some 4-5 people in your life who have established themselves and have become successful in the last few years.

Let's observe their life.

Let's observe their thought process.

Let's apply Spiral Theory in their life, you will understand it better.

> ***Successful people knowingly apply Spiral Theory to their life.***

***

VIII
Law Of
Attraction

***

Nature is an abundant source of energy; everything here is in abundance, and everything is for you and available to you. The air, water, mountains, sky, trees, sand, everything is lying in abundance, and you have all the right to access it in as much quantity as you want. Nobody can stop you.

We are created by nature, although we are physical, we are energy sources in actual. Therefore, we are in the best sync with nature.

We are always connected with nature in the same way as mobile is connected to the network tower.

Energy Fundamental

Energy cannot be created, nor destroyed, it can be transmitted from one place to another. Energy can change its form from potential energy to kinetic energy and vice versa. Nature's energy is for us and works in the most beneficial interest for us.

Focus is where the energy is.

Relation between sub conscious mind & the Nature

Nature (now, I would call her "mother nature") is waiting for us to provide whatever we want, and at the latest possible time.

Mother nature comes to know all our needs through our subconscious mind. Sub conscious requests mother nature, which mother nature fulfills in 100% and therefore, sub conscious and mother nature are always in synchronization.

Our subconscious mind and mother nature behave in the same pattern. Their language of communication is the same. Whatever is not understood to the subconscious is not understood to mother nature and vice versa.

Therefore, it is very important for us to understand the language of communication of mother nature or the language of subconscious mind, this will help us to understand the "Law of Attraction".

So, for convenience, wherever sub conscious term is used it would include mother nature as well and vice versa, please note.

The law of attraction depends on our capacity to attract mother nature whatever we want and whenever we want.

This chapter will help you to learn the language of nature for attracting things as and when required.

Nature may not provide whatever we claim.

Have you ever used a computer or a laptop,

Certainly yes,

Have you ever come across a situation where you have entered multiple commands together and now, the computer is confused, which command is to be serviced and which is not.

The computer is in the position of Dilemma.

The same thing happens in our life.

We order multiple tasks to our subconscious and want everything to be fulfilled at once.

The sub conscious starts acting and tries to carry out multiple executions.

These may be in the same direction or in a different direction.

Many a times, these instructions are canceled from each other.

For example, at one moment, you wanted to go to some place, or you want to carry out some tasks.

The sub conscious takes note of it and starts acting for the same and to your surprise, another moment, you think of not going to that place or you find negative thoughts coming about going to the certain place or carrying out certain tasks.

These thoughts could be like you might fail doing the said task, or it is not worth doing this task, resulting action happens at subconscious level but these being canceling thoughts, overall effect is nullified.

> *The subconscious religiously acts on all thoughts which occur in your mind, and everything is done without fail, just like earth's gravity pulls everything towards itself without fail.*

If the thoughts are not canceling thoughts, then there is another possibility of having multiple thoughts together i.e., issuing multiple instructions to subconscious mind all at once.

The subconscious starts taking actions on all tasks, but the energy gets scattered as all tasks are supposed to be done and the effect of the sub conscious action is not seen.

This has been reiterated earlier that everything that happens at a physical level initially starts happening at the mind / energy level.

Our thoughts are energy source and having multiple thoughts together i.e., issuing multiple instructions to sub conscious mind together will result scattered energy on sub conscious actions and thus the thoughts cannot become reality, or it take time to let them become a real thing.

> *The higher the energy, the higher the possibility of realizing the thought.*

Nature can provide whatever we feel.

We are all energy sources and everything around us is also a source of energy. People, animals, plants, human beings are physically a body, but at energy level, we are a source of energy only.

As said, whatever happens at physical level, first initiates at energy level and therefore, many things which start acting at energy level are not seen acting at physical level initially. We can see a physical change at a very later stage when physical changes happen.

This can be understood with the below examples.

- A large iceberg is floating over sea water. Sun rays are falling over it. There is no change physically and the Iceberg looking cool and calm. One day, Iceberg falls and drowns in the sea water.

What happened?

Iceberg was dissolving in the water constantly for the last many days, weeks or months although no physical change was observed.

It drowned one day as not able to hold itself. Though there is no physical change observed before the Iceberg got drowned, energy kept on changing its form from the day 1, and the ultimate physical change was the result of accumulated efforts of change brought to the Iceberg by energy.

- You can see water boiling in a bowl over an ignited gas stove. The flames are heating the bowl and the water. Initially, no change was observed physically. After some time, the water starts boiling. So, no physical change was observed during this time, but something was in the process and that change was brought to you by energy which the gas flame was putting in it.

I am sure I can let you understand that the physical changes which we see are the ultimate outcome of continuous efforts made by energy to change.

In the same way, our thoughts are a source of energy. Sub conscious process these thoughts to create things.

Thoughts Become Things

The subconscious can be imagined as an engine and thoughts can be its fuel. Without fuel, the engine cannot work. It's like you have high end car with you but the petrol tank is empty. You cannot drive it and take it to your home.

What is the value of this car? Is it worthful to you?

In the same way, your car has fuel, but the quantity is less, or the quality is not as per the desired level.

How the car will run, it cannot make a speed, or will not give you fuel efficiency, or the temperature of the vehicle will rise.

This is what we are doing with our body vehicle.

We are putting less energy thoughts in our sub conscious or various unstructured thoughts putting together letting sub conscious to confuse what to execute first.

>**Right Amount of Energy to be put for the thoughts to become Things.**

Feeling and Emotions bring energy to the thoughts.

For thoughts to become powerful, thoughts should be fueled with lots of feelings and emotions.

A happy feeling and a happy emotion will create a happy thought.

A sad feeling and a sad emotion will create a sad thought.

Mother nature does not understand good or bad.

Mother nature cannot differentiate between a good feeling or a bad feeling, you can say this is her weakness, but this is the way she operates.

Mother nature does not even understand what a happy feeling is or what a sad feeling is.

Yes, it can differentiate a feeling with deep feeling and a shallow feeling.

The Subconscious repeats deep feelings in life whatever it may be happy or sad. Like if you are deeply happy, sub conscious will try to arrange happiness for you in future and so a happy individual will become happier and happier over time.

In the same way, if you are deeply sad, sub conscious will try to arrange sad feelings for you in future and so a sad individual will become sadder over time.

Generally, sad feelings are deeper as we take sadness to the heart easily and therefore, a sad person becomes sadder easily.
You can say that this is the main cause of depression, anxiety and even suicides.

Let's put it in the form of an example for better understanding.

One will become very sad if he gets to know of bad news or something bad happens to him and sadness will be so much that his heart will be filled with bad feelings about the circumstance or for any person.

Let's change the situation,

Instantly, he got good news that the information, because of which he was sad, was wrong and there is nothing happened like this.

Now, observe his feelings.

Yes, he will be happy but noticing fact is that the depth of happy feeling will not be so strong as that of having a sad feeling.

This is the problem.

As said above, feelings and emotions bring energy to thoughts, these are fuels for thoughts to become things.

Since sad feelings are deeper emotions, they have more fuel and therefore, they have more probability to become real.

We NEED to eliminate them.

How to do it?

think

> **When you face difficulties, feel that challenges are not sent to destroy you. They are sent to build you and make you stronger.**

What to do Next?

Difficult situations shall be faced with a smile without putting unnecessary stress on your mind, body and soul.

AND

Try to search for happiness in every moment, making it deeper and happier.

Every small moment shall be celebrated with great happiness.

Mother nature does not understand tenses - Past or Future, it only understands PRESENT.

- Affirmations help to reinforce what already exists.

- Mother nature does not understand the past and future, it only understands present moment.

- LOA does not understand negatives, negative statements, NO /NOT statements, so affirmations should be made in the form of positive statements.

- Experience the feeling of your affirmation and acknowledge them.

- Try to do Visualization of affirmation, it helps.

- Sticking to one thought will focus all energy over a single thought and thus makes it a powerful affirmation.

- Every thought is acted upon by mother nature in the same way as gravity never forgets to pull things towards itself.

- Thoughts rightly presented to nature shall become things i.e., reality.

- Success time and success rate of fulfillment of desired thoughts depends on your focus as energy is where the focus is.

- Repetition is a must as practicing helps.

***

IX
Your Sub Conscious Mind

***

Let's understand how our sub conscious and conscious mind operate?

Physically there is one brain consisting of logical minds viz, Conscious Mind and Sub-conscious Mind.

Conscious mind does what we do consciously.

Our conscious thoughts and actions, like what we do, act, read, write consciously are all acts of our conscious mind.

Our subconscious mind does all remaining work which our conscious mind does not do.

Like, our breathing, flow of blood in our veins, like our nails and hairs grow, skin regenerates.

All our subconscious thoughts and sleep patterns are acts of our subconscious mind. These are some of the many thousand activities being done by sub conscious.

The conscious mind does 10% of total task and the rest 90% is done by our sub conscious mind.

See, subconscious mind does 9 times more tasks than our conscious mind.

Conscious Boss, Subconscious Servant

Conscious mind is the Boss, or the CEO of the institution and sub conscious is his team of servants or employees. Just like the Team serves the purpose of the CEO, acts for him, does all tasks assigned by him, in the same way, sub conscious acts to carry out instructions of conscious.

Key objective of the sub conscious is to carry out all tasks assigned by conscious mind. In short, it must keep its Boss happy.

The power of sub consciousness is unimaginable. It can do anything unbelievable. It can create or destroy anything. It can be as creative as mother nature and at the same time it can be as destructive as mother nature.

It can create Mother Teresa, to relieve all pain and bring happiness in the life of mankind. It can also create a Hitler to serve his ugly dreams. It can bring out Mahatma or a buddha or a Mahavira out of you to lead on the path of truth and non-violence.

It can make you a Sadhu and give you enlightenment or can make you Jeff Bezos or Warren Buffet.

Obama and Osama both are created by it.

Whatever you wanted to take out of it, you will be. This is your choice.

There is no limitation on anything because everything is in abundance in the territory of mother nature.

Mother nature is more powerful than a supercomputer and more knowledgeable than Google.

All inventions and discoveries of the world are made by human beings and certainly by their subconscious.

Just like everything in this world has a certain style of doing things.

Same way, sub conscious has its own way of doing things.

We need to learn and understand the language of its communication for it to be most beneficial for us.

Let's have it.

Abundance V/s Scarcity Mindset

As said, sub conscious works as a servant of conscious and carry out its instructions. It works to make conscious happier.

How it works?

Let's say, conscious is thinking to do something bad for somebody.

What sub conscious will do?

It will start to act on the thought.

What will happen?

Certainly, bad things will start coming to you.

But it has weaknesses as well,

The subconscious understands feelings and emotions but does not differentiate between happy feeling and a sad feeling.

Yes, it can differentiate between deep feeling and a shallow feeling.

Sad feelings are generally deep feelings and therefore, once the subconscious knows that the conscious is in a particular feeling, subconscious starts creating the same feeling for it in more quantity.

The subconscious will create happy feelings for you if you are happy consciously and vice versa.

The subconscious understands deep feelings more than shallow feelings.

So, this is for those who want to be happier. They must create deep feelings of happiness.

Act of fooling around subconscious

The subconscious has one more weakness, you can say.

It does not differentiate between real and fake. It does not differentiate between an actual picture or a visual image.

If you create a deep feeling of beautiful house wherein you wish to live in and you create a visual image of it. You create an impression that you are getting your dream house, and you are visualizing its color, shape, size, design, its rooms, kitchen, garden and the facilities which it has.

Your visual image should be so clear that it looks like a real one.

Key reason for failures, delays in the path of success

The subconscious will start acting to create this visual thought of yours into THINGS,

and one day,

it is certain that the very same house that you visual it will be yours.

The sub conscious has the capability of doing anything, no doubt about it and Every thought is acted upon by it without fail.

Like gravitational force cannot forget to attract underlying object to pull towards it, same way, subconscious do not forget to act upon any thought or action created by conscious, whether good or bad.

Then why failure and delays?

As said, conscious acts as a Master and subconscious act as a Servant.

At times, it happens, Master gives instruction to the Servant, instantly another thought gets created counteracting the first action or a doubt gets created in the mind of Master.

The doubt can be on the capabilities or worthiness, whatever, but doubt is doubt.

This confuses the subconscious.

And the result is neutralized.

What is required to avoid failures and delays?

One should avoid doubts and negativities in its subconscious thoughts and actions to avoid failures.

Delays in results can be avoided by creating deeper feelings, as repeated deep feelings will authenticate the results much faster.

Sub conscious actions in life

1. Sub conscious effect on physical body

If one is having fever and is taken to the doctor of his choice. The doctor gives him some medicine saying that he will be fine within a few days. The patient takes the medicine for the prescribed duration and gets cured. This is the placebo effect.

In the same way, if the patient is not confident about the doctor's ability to cure him then certainly, he will not be cured even if the right medicines are prescribed to him.

This is a subconscious effect which has been brought to us by ensuring us that the doctor has the capability of curing this disease and has provided us with the right medication.

This sub conscious action of the mind helps us get out of illness.

2. Sub conscious effect on mindset

If you are searching for something lying in any drawer etc., without having the knowledge or confidence of that thing being there.

If you are not confident that you will get that thing at that place,

You will search but you will not get the thing, even if it is lying in front of you. You will miss eyesight on the thing placed just in front of you.

But when you have confidence and information that you will find the required item at a particular place, you will be easily able to search for that thing, and you easily get the thing. You can say sub conscious is working in some way in your mind.

3. Sub conscious connection with Success

Self-Doubt- Having self-doubt on the occurrence of anything is a sure way to failure, even if hardest efforts are put over it.

So, while doing something, one should be sure enough to get the things done successfully.

Self-doubt should be used as tool to recheck to verify the completeness of the task instead of creating a self-doubt on achievement of success.

Remember, whenever in the past, you have created self-doubt on achievement of success, you failed.

Worthiness - Unworthiness is another form of self-doubt. If one is feeling himself as unworthy to get something or feeling that the occurrence of something in his life will not be worth much. This is a self-doubt on his capabilities or a self-doubt on value addition in life on account of happening of the event, which is always an hinderance in the path of success.

A positive sub conscious action remains with confident individuals who do not have self-doubt or issues of unworthiness, leading them to success.

***

X
How To Let Our Dreams Come True

Our dreams are suffering from negativities and limiting beliefs.

Negativities relate to self-worth.

People think they want to have something, but they do not deserve it.

If one does not deserve it, how can it be with him or her.

<u>How it happens, let's see</u>

One moment you thought of doing something, another moment a thought comes to your mind, finding difficulties in doing the very same task, next moment, you reach the outcome of the task and find it as you do not deserve it or it's not worth doing it. After spending some time, you come up with a decision to leave the task.

You do not deserve it or it's not worth doing it both are same in various parlances.

Limiting Beliefs

Limiting Beliefs are also negative in another perspective.

Here we are accepting things, we are not finding any difficulty in getting the task done, everything looking within our control of action, we think, we deserve it as well but with a different tendency.

If somebody thinks, he can earn Rs 1 L per day but cannot feel good to accumulate Rs 300 L in a year.

If the other person thinks, he can earn Rs 1K per day but cannot feel good to earn Rs 1 L per day.

Limiting beliefs are hurdles in the path of success & therefore, THINK BIG concept has its significance.

THINK BIG CONCEPT

While doing so, we should not have any limitation on the quantum & size of the wish.

Do not allow your conscious to create any DOUBT on the occurrence of the event, be conscious and be happy.

***

XI
Repetition-
A Way of Life

***

People get bored with repetitive tasks, they want something different, that's what I heard from lots of people.

I have a different view.

***Repetition is not boredom, it
is the way of life, mother nature
also does this.***

We start our day, wake up from bed, brush our teeth, clean our body – All that is repetition.

We eat food thrice a day, breakfast, lunch and dinner- a repetition.

We go to the office /business/shop daily in the morning, reaching the very same destination, sitting on the same chair, working on the same computer.

We do entertainment every week, go to movies, relax on holidays, meet, and greet friends, with approximately the same people, many times - again repetition.

Sun daily rises from the east, moon comes in the evening, every 15 days moon cycle changes.

The plants and trees grow daily.

our hairs, nails and skin grow daily, our ageing happens uniformly and equally every day.

Every year at the same time rain comes, season comes, winter, summer happens. Even plants and animals have a life cycle, water has cycle of change AND everything happening from millions of years and contains repetition.

Don't be afraid of it.

It is the way of mother nature, it is the way of life, it is the path of our ecological development.

Repeating each task increases its finesse, but all that is possible if we take interest in it.

Repetition is boring if it is disinteresting.

Repetition is enjoyable if it is interesting.

Therefore, we must find interest in it.

Any task can be interesting if we find uniqueness in its repetition.

Observe...

Everything which is repetitive has a uniqueness in it, there is something which is making it different from the previous one.

There is something new to learn from it and you will surprise to note that every task done will be better than the previous one, even if it is a repeat.

Our brain has 100 billion neurons, and they create bonds while doing the same act multiple times and thus our behavior and habits are developed.

To have a perfect life, our mind, body, and soul should be in sync, all that should be in sync with mother nature.

Our conscious mind and sub-conscious mind should be in sync.

Synchronization comes with repetition. It gives us less resistance, so less pain.

Resistance is the main cause of pain.

What happens if we want to flow in a direction opposite to the direction of water flowing in the river.

We would have to face maximum resistance and maximum pain occurs to come out of it.

If we decide to flow with the flow of water and surrender ourselves to it. There will be less resistance, less pain.

This is the most appropriate position of Synchronization.

But you can sync once you are confident of your safety and existence then only you can surrender yourself.

This confidence can only be built only after repeated practice of flowing in the same river water, multiple times, in the very same scenario.

Repetition is therefore mandatory – Accept it.

Repetition V/s Practice

We have heard of professionals doing practice.

Doctors daily go to the clinic, see patients, give medicines, do surgeries, all of a repeated nature, same diseases, same medicines and same surgeries for different people on daily basis. Doctors do it regularly and for years.

Same way, Chartered Accountants, Advocates, engineers, film stars, directors, producers, artists, painters, musicians, singers everybody do their same routine processes on daily basis, and they call it as "Practice."

Professionals are valued by their seasoning of practice.

Practice gives them experience and one would want to get consulted with a professional who has several years of experience of practice for their kind of requirement.

Practice is doing task repetitively.

***

XII

Theory of Vibration

Even if you have a high-end Maserati car, you cannot make it run if it does not have sufficient fuel of the right quality.

Your thoughts are your Maserati and Vibration is its fuel.

The initial chapters of the book were more focused on understanding thoughts.

Why?

Because we understood

1.   Mind, Body, and Soul & Importance of their synchronization.
2.   Conscious and Sub Conscious Mind and their connection,
3.   Universe and its connection with Sub Conscious.
4.   Power of the Thoughts
5.   Habits and Behavior
6.   Law of Attraction, Pineal Gland etc.

Now, it is time to put fuel into it to make it run as per our wishes.

We know everything whether it is a living being or a non-living thing, if we crash into the smallest particle, the last unbreakable portion is a "Cell" which cannot be broken further.

These cells cannot be seen with naked eyes, these can be seen with high end microscopic cameras.

If we study Molecular Physics, we come to know that a cell in physical body whether living or a nonliving, it is into vibration state.

No matter if it is in solid, or liquid or gas form, the cells remain in vibration mode.

Even our heart beats, blood pumps in and out, Pulse vibrate.

Vibration is on account of having kinetic energy in the cell or we can say, since the cell is having kinetic energy in it, is vibrating.

This applies to our thoughts as well.

Energy helps vibrate the thoughts.

The higher the energy, the higher the vibration.

Higher energy and high vibration work as a quality fuel for thoughts to become things.

This is the reason why some dreams of some people happen and within lesser period of time because they put appropriate quality and quantity of vibration energy to their right thoughts.

Some people, even after having the right thoughts with them cannot succeed in their accomplishment which is on account of lack of right vibration energy.

What is low & high vibration energy?

Negative vibration thoughts creating low vibration energy.

1. Anguish, revengeful, opportunistic, greedy, proud, ugly, and biased thoughts
2. Low feeling, depressive, diminishing, destructive thoughts.
3. Fearful and Sad thoughts
4. Thoughts of fight
5. Runaway thoughts
6. Step back thoughts

7.	Thoughts of disaster
8.	Erotic, vulgar, and bad thoughts

[Please don't get confused with my previous statement and current remarks.

For clarity,

Negative thoughts have low vibration energy but since we take these negative thoughts very close to our heart and do them repetitively, the energy of these negative low vibration thoughts gets increased.
This is the reason why efficiency rate of negative thoughts are more than positive thoughts,

Hope I it is clarified now.]

Positive vibration thoughts creating high vibration energy.

1.	Thoughts of happiness, cheer, unbiased, non-aggressive, friendly, loving, caring, beauty.
2.	Thoughts of gratitude
3.	Creative, inventive, and innovative thoughts
4.	Upgrading thoughts
5.	Be good and have good thoughts.
6.	Easy thought, relax thought.
7.	Thought of hard work or smart work
8.	Step Forward thought.
9.	Love and Romantic thought

10. Spiritual thoughts
11. Knowledge thought
12. Thoughts of enjoyment
13. Helpful & Supportive thoughts
14. Righteous thoughts

How do we get high vibration energy?

High vibration energy can be obtained by -

1. Avoiding low vibration thoughts
2. Allowing high vibration thoughts.

High vibration energy can be obtained by adopting following in your lifestyle.

• **Meditation**

Meditation helps in synchronization of Mind, Body, and Soul. Meditation reduces chattering in the mind and thus reduces cluttering of thoughts. It allows focused and unidirectional thoughts.

Energy is where the focus is.

Focused thought inputs energy at the focused point and stops scattering of energy. It is just like a lens putting over paper in sunlight, burns the paper in seconds.

This is because all sunlight falling over the lens centers at the focus point and together burns the paper.

Meditation creates high vibration energy and works as a fuel on unidirectional focused thoughts.

Why unidirectional?

Meditation creates sync between Mind, Body and Soul, establishes relationship between conscious and sub conscious mind, it allows positive thoughts and eliminates negative and countervailing thoughts. Thus, thoughts become conscious and unidirectional.

- **Yoga Asanas**
- **Right Food habits**
- Eliminate alcohol and smoke.
- Eliminate nonveg from your diet
- **Being happy**
- **Paying gratitude**
- **Start your day with positive thoughts.**

***

XIII
Pineal Gland

The agenda of this book is to understand the science of your thoughts, creatively beautifying them and getting productive use of it.

Understanding the importance of Pineal Gland is quite related and immensely important.

So, let's focus.

Pineal gland, a pea shaped, rice grain sized gland in the brain, situated in the deep center, straight to eyes, also called as Third Eye.

Pineal produces Serotonin and Melatonin

Serotonin, also called happy chemical, helps brain cells and nervous cells to communicate with each other, regulates sleeping, eating and digestion. Low Serotonin leads to depression, anxiety, and sleep trouble.

Melatonin is responsible for regulating sleep patterns, it is secreted in the night to allow us to sleep, Lack of Melatonin causes sleeplessness, in turn, stress, anxiety etc.

It also manages fertility and menstrual system in females.

Serotonin is secreted in the day, wakes us up and activates our life, Melatonin is secreted in the night, helps us to sleep.

What is Activation of Pineal?

Pineal is coated with calcium, decalcifying it will activate it.

Avoid Calcification?

Calcified pineal gland disturbs sleep, reduces reaction time, judgment, cognitive abilities, and performance.

Decalcification is required at least to avoid Calcification.

- Excess of Chlorine & Fluorine chemicals may calcify it creating harmful effects.

- Therefore, first, it is important to avoid these chemicals like chloride and fluoride waters are first cleaned before use.

- You have seen yellow teeth of people living in villages which is mostly because of excess use of chloride and fluoride waters.

Use appropriate Reverse Osmosis (RO) or Carbon block water purifiers ensuring complete elimination of these chemicals out of water.

Doctors generally prescribe calcium syrups and tablets, this being synthetic calcium, reaches body, excess calcium remained after use is left over in the blood which moves to various organs of the body, may reach Pineal and calcify it.

Many companies happily advertise Fluoride toothpastes, not a healthy item for Pineal.

How is Activation done?

Pineal is sensitive to light. Since it is situated straight to the eyes, light can easily reach it. Hence, Sun gazing in the morning and evening, can be an easier option for activation. Meditation, Yoga, and certain food supplements may help activation of Pineal over a period.

Why Activation required?

In addition to other benefits, activation of Pineal gives synchronization between conscious and sub conscious mind.

If you are feeling pressure at the center of your forehead, between your eyebrows then this is a good symptom of your Pineal being activated.

Note: Activation of pineal gland (third eye) should be done in the presence of an expert.

***

XIV
Visualization Exercises

This section of the book is a practical guide on how to develop positive thoughts and how to manifest them through the process of Visualization.

Visualization is the most effective method of Law of Attraction and Manifestation.

You are provided with a set of daily exercises to carry out regularly.

Certainly, there are few rules to be followed -

1. One exercise at a time
2. First exercise shall be taken first.
3. Next exercise shall be taken up once the first exercise gets completed.
4. Don't read, even don't see the next exercise unless the previous one gets completed. Let it come as a surprise.
5. Doing it regularly.
6. Practicing it as much as you can.
7. Stick to the rules as much as possible.

***

XV
Affirmation
Exercises

Basic Level Affirmations

It is recommended to remember these affirmations at least 3 times a day for at least 21 days.

Repeat following Affirmations daily. It is very good to do it more than that.

While doing so, one should have a happy energetic feeling and try to visualize it as much as possible.

1. I am abundant.
2. I am happy.
3. I am healthy.
4. I am rich.
5. My bank balance is increasing day by day.
6. I have ample time for me and my family.
7. I am becoming healthier day by day.
8. My family's health is improving day by day.
9. My love for my family and friends is increasing day by day.
10. I am feeling happier and happier day by day.
11. I am feeling relaxed and comfortable.
12. I am doing my best.
13. I am worthy.
14. I am free from Worries and Regrets.
15. I am talented and Intelligent.
16. I am beautiful.
17. I am kind.
18. I am a money magnet.
19. I am a wealth magnet.
20. I am a love magnet.

You can create your Affirmations as well.

We can go to higher level affirmations once; we practice this for 21 days. We can do it for more time to let ourselves proficient at this level. Proficiency at this level will determine success at higher levels.

Higher Level Affirmations

Higher level affirmations are affirmations with a clear set of goals to be achieved within specified duration.

We will learn high level affirmations in the coming editions.

***